PRACTICAL PRINCESS
perfect wardrobe

PRACTICAL PRINCESS
perfect wardrobe

Declutter and re-jig your
closet to transform your life

Elika Gibbs

photography by Polly Wreford

RYLAND
PETERS
& SMALL
London New York

Senior designer: Sonya Nathoo
Senior Editor: Annabel Morgan
Picture research: Emily Westlake
Head of Production: Patricia Harrington
Art Director: Leslie Harrington
Publishing Director: Alison Starling

Published in 2011 by Ryland Peters & Small
20–21 Jockey's Fields, London WC1R 4BW
519 Broadway, 5th Floor, New York NY 10012

www.rylandpeters.com

10 9 8 7 6 5 4 3 2 1

A CIP record for this book is available from the
British Library.

Library of Congress cataloging-in-publication data has
been applied for

ISBN: 978 1 84975 114 8

Printed in China

contents

introduction

The following pages contain the tried-and-tested Practical Princess formula that I use at work every day. I work with a myriad of clients whose individual needs are many and varied, and so I tailor each job slightly to benefit them. Some clients will only require wardrobe organization, while others need to go through the full process of assessment, organization and shopping.

I do not claim to be a fashionista in any way, shape or form, but I have had the privilege to work with many fashion icons. My unique formula has worked for each and every one of them, as they have been able to get clarity in their vast wardrobes.

By following these steps, I hope that you too will achieve 'closet clarity' and enjoy getting dressed again.

the practical princess story

Practical Princess evolved and grew without me actually even knowing it. It didn't begin in the conventional way that a lot of companies do. I didn't have a vision, and certainly didn't have a business plan, but this is the story of how it all started.

In my late twenties, I opened up a designer and couture evening dress hire shop in Knightsbridge, London, with my then business partner Arabella Bodie. Our aim was to have a shop where you could hire a beautiful long gown for the night without having to spend thousands of pounds buying a dress you might only wear once. We stocked gorgeous dresses from designers such as Bruce Oldfield, Amanda Wakeley, Jenny Packham and Vera Wang. Ladies could also hire jewellery, shoes, handbags and pashminas, making it a one-stop shop.

We also sold the original 'Magic Knickers'. These had not yet hit the market – Arabella and I had sourced them from a European trade fair – and they became a great hit. They were so popular that at times we would sit up all night packing hundreds of pairs of knickers to send out worldwide.

After running the shop for a number of years, our lives started to change. Arabella got married and – whoops! – I got pregnant. Becoming a single mum and Arabella leaving Bodie & Gibbs had a dramatic effect upon my life. Financially, with a baby to support, I was finding it hard to survive on the salary that I drew. I had to find a way to earn more money.

Whether by luck, fate or perfect timing, I was asked by a successful and busy executive to help organize and restructure her household. I was hesitant about accepting the offer, as I had no training or qualifications in this field, but I was assured that I could do it and I really needed the extra cash. Although I was still running the shop, during the next couple of years I spent a day a week reorganizing every nook and cranny of her home, from kitchen cupboards to wardrobes. I also helped hire and train her staff, and shopped for anything from bed linens to new pairs of jeans. You name it, I did it!

At this point my main focus was still Bodie & Gibbs. Over the years, I had built some wonderful relationships with a number of clients who I would regularly dress for parties and events. I have always been one to push the boundaries, and I had encouraged many of them to move out of their comfort zone and try something different. I was flattered when they started to ask me to help them with their day-to-day look too, and this was how I started personal shopping.

Not all personal shoppers will look at a client's wardrobe before they shop, but for me it was a logical step, so that I could see what clothes they had and what was missing. I was often shocked to discover the way in which these ladies kept their clothes. No wonder they couldn't get dressed! I realized that these women were not the unstylish, hopeless cases that they thought.

In fact, some had wonderful pieces lurking in the depths of their wardrobe but that were just not getting used.

I realized that I couldn't help my clients or take them shopping until I could get 'closet clarity'. And this is where my formula began to develop. I didn't want to humiliate or embarrass anyone, but I needed them to try on their clothes so that we could establish what worked and what didn't. By rehanging and reorganizing their closets, we were able to establish the gaps that needed to be filled when we went shopping.

I guess that this is when Practical Princess started to take form. It slowly evolved and grew by word of mouth, and bookings began to include household and office moves. Thankfully, all the knowledge and know-how I had obtained from running my shop, along with the new experiences gained from different clients' needs, helped me to take on these new challenges. Fearful as I was to take the next step, as my livelihood and that of my little girl depended upon it, I decided to close the door on my dress shop and concentrate on making Practical Princess my full-time profession.

That was five years ago, and even though there have been trials and tribulations, tears and laughter, my business has expanded and I now have 'princesses' who run their own teams. I have developed my own product range and opened a storage centre for my clients to store off-season and archive clothes.

On reflection, I wonder whether I would have had the foresight and courage to start Practical Princess if I had not been in dire straits. I certainly felt the fear, but I didn't have the time to think about the consequences if things went wrong, and for that I am grateful.

I now consider myself so lucky to love what I do for a living. The variety and challenges that face me day to day are never boring, and I have met some amazing people along the way who have been instrumental in supporting me. New opportunities and ventures are again being placed in front of me – this book being one. The fear came back, but it was a challenge I couldn't resist!

wardrobe
assessment

does your wardrobe reflect your life?

The Practical Princess process always starts the same way, with a consultation to meet my client face to face in their own environment. This is to help me build a picture of the client, so that when I look through their wardrobe I can see whether their clothes reflect their lifestyle. I ask my clients to tell me a bit about themselves while I gently question them to get the answers I need. I want you to ask yourself the same questions:

- Do you work?
- How do you spend your days?
- What's your marital status?
- Are you a parent?
- What's your social life?
- Do you have any upcoming events?
- What are your interests?
- Do you travel?
- Are you happy with your weight and well-being?
- Have you had any life-changing events/circumstances?
- Where do you live and what's the climate?

By answering these questions you should be able to see whether your wardrobe reflects your lifestyle. Let me give you an example, but don't try and identify with the character, as this is purely to illustrate why this process is vital.

One of my clients is a forty-something female, divorced from a wealthy banker and with no children. She was having a crisis. Her old life required her to wear dresses and suits that, she said, 'made her feel like the mother of the bride'. However, her life had dramatically changed. She was about to embark on a new career where the dress code boundary was blurred. Having been single

for a few years, she had developed a crush on a younger man and desperately wanted to become a cougar! Her holidays were always spent with her family, who still expected her to conform, and her self-worth was on the floor. She was in desperate need of help. She felt she had no sense of style, no longer knew who she was and was struggling to get dressed in the morning.

When I looked through her wardrobe, I could see that her old and new lives were all tangled up. There was the normal wardrobe chaos that I always see, but from a psychological point of view she had not yet let go of her old life.

By going through her wardrobe garment by garment, she began to see that more than half her clothes were no longer relevant to her life. A smile finally spread over her face as she realized that it was not because she had no style, but because she had changed as a woman. This gave her the encouragement she needed to continue with my process. What people don't seem to realize is that their clothes can tie them to an identity that is stuck in the past.

trying on

A proper assessment takes longer than expected, so don't dive in hoping to sort out your wardrobe in a couple of hours on a Saturday morning. You either need to set aside a proper chunk of time – such as a whole weekend – or break the tasks down into bite-size pieces by doing all your skirts one evening, all your trousers another.

STEP BY STEP

I don't want you to try all of your clothes on just as they come out of your wardrobe – this will quickly become overwhelming and you may just give up! I find that if I stick with one garment type at a time, it keeps my clients focused and the process is much more successful. The repetition of trying on the same item of clothing over and over allows them to make a good comparison of style and fit. This gives my clients the confidence and ability to continue the process later on their own. If you do the same, it will be easier for you to gauge what to get rid of and what to keep.

Breaking clothes down into sub-sections will help you even more. Let me give you an example: if you are working on trousers, put them into categories – jeans, combats, tailored trousers and so on – as this will give you an idea of how many similar pairs you have and which is the better fit.

If you find that you have, say, five pairs of black trousers, are there some that you have not worn for a while or perhaps never wear? A lot of my clients hang onto trousers because they think that they are timeless. Yet trousers seem to date quicker than anything else. This is why it is so important to try everything on and take the time to look at yourself properly in a full-length mirror.

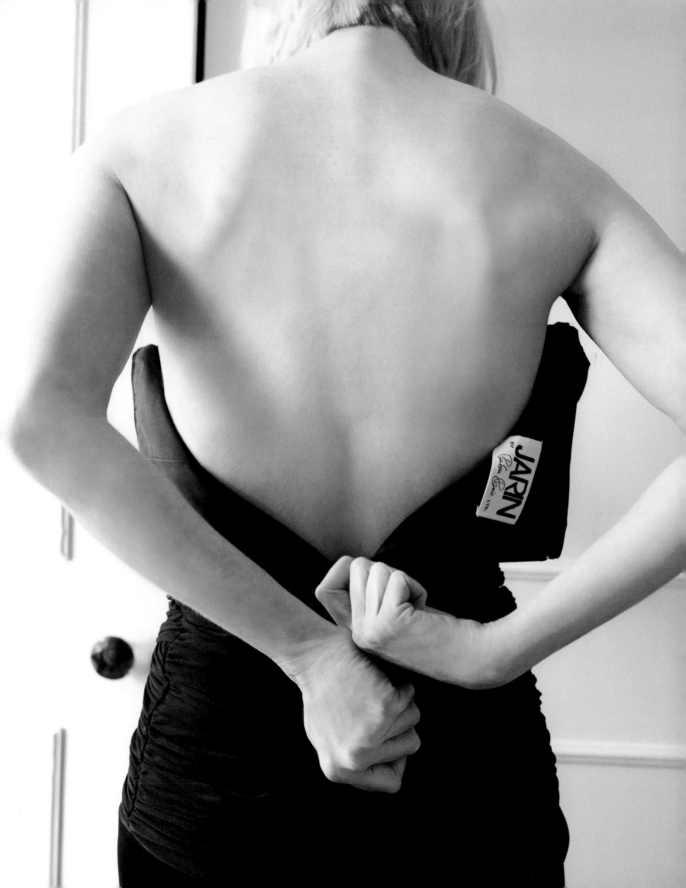

the six-pile process

As you try on your clothes, you will need to create six piles to help you keep order throughout the process. I often use sticky notes to mark my piles, so that items don't get mixed up.

1 KEEP

The fit and the look are working for you.

There must be no question mark hanging over these items. They must look good, fit well and be in good condition. They must also be relevant to your lifestyle, as identified in your wardrobe assessment. At the end of this exercise, don't panic if this is your smallest pile. You haven't gone wrong; you are simply being realistic about what does and doesn't look good. You must trust in this process, or you will not benefit from my tried-and-tested formula.

2 ARCHIVE

Pieces that you no longer wear, but don't want to part with.

Of course, there are always pieces that we want to hang onto, and archiving clothes allows us to return to and reuse things at a later date. I have kept some cherished pieces that I can no longer wear for my little girl. You may also have items that you want to hand down to someone special. Having said all of this, you still have to be realistic about how much you keep and where you are going to store it. If you are not wearing it, you shouldn't see it!

3 MAYBE

Your headache pile: should it stay or should it go?

When you are umming and ahhing over an item, there are a few important things to consider. Does it fit? Is it flattering? Is the cut, shape or detail dated? For instance, even if you don't have a good pair of jeans to put in your KEEP pile, don't be scared to get rid of unflattering pairs. It is better to have a gap in your wardrobe that you can fill when you go shopping. This will help you to buy what you need and stop impulse buying. When the gaps are identified, you strip away the illusion of having a complete wardrobe with loads of clothes yet nothing to wear. Does this sound familiar?

4 EDIT

Things to move on, including mistakes, wrong sizes or worn-out items.

The key to editing successfully is brutal honesty. We have all made a fashion faux pas (or two) and later destroyed the photographic evidence. With hindsight, remortgaging the house to buy that fabulous dress was clearly a mistake! Just because something is designer or expensive doesn't give it the privilege to sit in your wardrobe. This pile should also contain clothes that are tired, worn out or over-laundered. There's nothing worse than a dingy off-white vest, even if it is one of your day-to-day basic pieces that you might be reluctant to throw away. These wardrobe basics need to be continually edited and replaced.

5 DRY-CLEANING, LAUNDRY AND ALTERATIONS

Very Important!

There is nothing worse than going to put something on only to find it needs to be dry-cleaned or laundered. Equally annoying is when you have planned an outfit and then realize that a zip is broken or a seam has come undone. Make sure that your clothes are always ready to wear. Don't put dirty or damaged pieces into your wardrobe until they have been dealt with.

Often, dated clothes can be modernized with a simple alteration. It is amazing what a difference simply changing a hemline or swapping the buttons can make to an outfit. So put items that can be updated on this pile.

6 SEASONAL CHANGEOVER

The clothes that you wear in the depth of winter or the height of summer should be packed away for the reverse season. Doing this will create space in your wardrobe and help you identify any gaps.

The six-pile process may seem over the top and a waste of time, but if you stick to this tried-and-tested formula, I promise the benefits will be endless.

what to do with your edit pile

CAR BOOT/YARD SALE

This is probably my favourite way of moving on my edit pile as well as any unwanted household and family items. Not everyone may relish getting up at the crack of dawn to sell their unwanted possessions, but personally I get a real buzz from them! By trial and error I have honed my sales technique. I did no preparation at all for my first sale and started off with plastic bags full of clothes and a trestle table. Of course I ended up in chaos, underselling a lot of my items, as I could not display them adequately. I learned from this experience and realized that I needed to put into practice the basic formula I use at work. As ever, organization is the key.

The next time, I put prime items onto hangers and placed bags, shoes and toys in plastic tubs. I knew this would help me set up my stall quickly and efficiently. The effect that I wanted this time was not that of a jumble sale but a well-arranged, enticing stall, giving me a platform to sell more and in turn make more cash. I am happy to report that this time I was successful!

Here are some tools and tips that helped me:
• Hangers (this is the *only* time that wire ones are allowed!)
• Hanging rail
• Trestle/wallpaper table
• Baskets, boxes, plastic tubs
• Plastic bags for sold items
• Money belt (stocked with plenty of change)
• Plastic sheeting to cover your items in case it rains
• A friend to give you moral support
• Wear layered clothing, as the early mornings can be cold
• Tidy up your stall in the quiet periods
• Be realistic with pricing – you are there to sell, not to bring things back home
• Don't bring unsold items back into the house – take them straight to the local charity shop/thrift store

EBAY

Pretty much anything can be sold on eBay, due to its huge global audience. For some people it is easy and very profitable, but for others it is time-consuming with little reward.

Each item you want to sell has to be photographed in several different ways, showing as much detail as possible. A written description is also required, providing measurements and any other relevant details. The more information you give, the less time you will need to spend answering buyer's enquiries.

Ebay have strict rules and regulations to protect their buyers and only give you five working days to ship the goods after payment is received. Send parcels and packages by recorded mail, as your item will then be insured and can be tracked.

I am hopeless at the eBay process because I don't have the time or patience needed. However, I do recognize eBay's selling potential, so my company, Practical Princess, uses it to sell designer pieces that clients no longer want.

RESALE SHOPS

There are more and more resale shops cropping up all over the place. It is important to do your research before you choose a shop, as they all have different criteria. Here are some questions you should ask:
• Do they only take designer labels?
• Do the clothes have to be dry-cleaned and in impeccable condition?
• What percentage do they take from the selling price?
• Do they take off-season clothes?
• How long after an item is sold are you paid? And what form does payment take?
• What happens to any unsold items?

CHARITY/THRIFT STORES

If you can afford to, or have a heart of gold, the best way to get rid of your edit pile is to give it to charity.

The easiest route is a quick drop at your local charity shop/thrift store. If you can't find one that supports your favourite charity, you could do the same as some of my clients. They sell their clothes through resale or eBay then donate the proceeds to their chosen cause.

If you can afford to, or have a heart of gold, the best way to get rid of your edit pile is to give it to charity.

what to do with your unwanted clothes

	PROS	CONS
CAR BOOT/ YARD SALE	• All the profit is yours • Likely to sell all unwanted items • You get some fresh air	• Haggling with punters over small change will drive you mad • Might not get as much money as you hoped per item. • Early start!
RESALE SHOP	• Little effort required • Competitively priced	• 40–60% commission charged • Off-season garments not always taken • Labels are selected at shop's discretion
EBAY	• Worldwide audience • Can get people bidding up on items	• Time-consuming, in all aspects: photographing, corresponding with bidders, packaging & posting and returns • Fees • Unless you have a minimum reserve price, you could end up with pennies • Getting your ratings up so that people trust you takes time
CHARITY/ THRIFT STORE	• Recycling • Helping others • Everything taken	• Getting it there • It is unhelpful and in some places illegal to leave donations outside the shop (out of hours)

storage

In my late teens and early twenties I moved from flat to flat, not caring or worrying about how my clothes were packed or stored. I was forever giving my parents boxes and cases of things I wanted them to keep for me. When I eventually opened them years later, it was soul-destroying to see the damage that damp and moths had caused. I wish I had known then what I know now – how a few simple steps could have saved my clothes.

Most of the time we have little choice as to where we store our archive, but it is imperative that we choose a damp- and sunlight-free zone. Any places that suffer from extreme temperature swings should be avoided, as should badly ventilated or uninsulated attics, basements and garages.

Your storage space will determine what you store your clothes in. Most of us have to store items in boxes or suitcases, since it is rare to find spare hanging space. It is preferable to use specialized cardboard dress boxes because they are not completely airtight, enabling the garments to breathe. It is also very important that you launder or dry-clean all clothes before they are stored. If something has been worn, even if it looks and smells clean, there will be skin cells and sweat left on the garment that will inevitably attract moths.

Before you start packing, wash your hands so that you do not transfer skin oils onto the clothes. Line the box with acid-free tissue paper. The trick is to make sure that you lay or fold each garment properly. The fewer folds you make, the better. Creases can become permanent on certain fabrics, and this should be avoided at all costs.

Each garment will require different care. Wedding dresses, ball gowns and other special items will need their own boxes and extra care should be taken when packing them. Acid-free tissue paper should be interleaved between folds, and crumpled tissue paper used to stuff the sleeves and bodice.

PRACTICAL PRINCESS

Givenchy

PRACTICAL PRINCESS

Givenchy

This will help to keep the shape, prevent creasing and ensure the longevity of your garments. If you are packing a number of items in one box, the same principle applies: interleave each garment when folding and use extra sheets of tissue paper to separate them. Some fabrics, trimmings and buttons may need to be treated differently. Metal buttons should be wrapped in acid-free tissue paper or even removed, as they can corrode and leave a nasty stain on fabric. When storing shoes, bags and accessories, make sure that you use acid-free tissue paper to wrap and stuff the bags.

If you are going to hang stored clothes, it is best to use breathable hanging garment bags. I use these in my storage centre for clients who do not have enough space to archive all their clothes. They protect garments from rubbing against one another or snagging. The bags are wide and long enough to prevent creasing, and a little space is left between each garment so that they are not all jammed together.

A moth deterrent must be placed in each box or bag. Slip this in between the sheets of tissue paper to avoid contact with the garments. They must be changed regularly, on average every three to six months. Replacing the moth repellent gives you a chance to check that the clothes are still in good condition.

CATALOGUING

I recommend that you photograph any item that you are storing for a long period of time. I photograph each garment on a mannequin and insert the picture in the dress bag pocket. When storing items in boxes, I create a written and photographic inventory of what's inside. This may seem unnecessary, but it is surprising how quickly we forget what we have packed away. It also makes it quick and easy to locate an item when it is needed.

SHORT-TERM STORAGE

I prefer to have only the current season's clothes hanging in a wardrobe. Of course, this is dependent on space, but if you can separate your summer and winter clothes, you will find it a lot easier to get dressed (note that I have not mentioned spring or autumn clothes, as these are usually transitional pieces that will carry us into the next season).

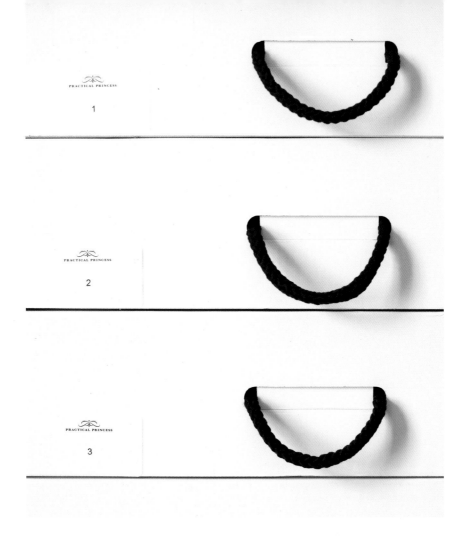

What to put away at the end of each season:

• Heavy winter coats. Shoulder covers will protect them against dust, saving on dry-cleaning bills.

• Pack up your resort wear, as you will only be wearing it on holiday. You don't want kaftans and sun hats mixed up with your day-to-day wear.

• Ski wear can be put into vacuum bags. This is not my favourite way of storing clothes, but it is extremely economical on space.

• Knits that you won't be wearing until next season can be stored in a variety of ways: plastic boxes, vacuum bags and sweater bags, or simply folded and piled on a high shelf at the top of your wardrobe.

• Note that if you are using vacuum bags for storage, steaming will be necessary before you use them again.

the cataloguing process

Red-carpet moments, gala balls and charity events all require dresses that scream drama. Unfortunately, they have a very short lifespan.

Clients of mine who are in the public eye tend not to be able to wear these dresses more than a few times, as they are constantly photographed. For these clients we create garment catalogues with several purposes. They are either to provide an archive record, for insurance purposes or for people with multiple homes, so that items are quick to locate should they need them.

| Christian Dior | Derek Lam | DVF | DVF |

| Gucci | Julien MacDonald | Kaat Tilley | Luca Luca |

Marchesa Notte

Matthew Williamson

Oscar de la Renta

Reem Acra

Reem Acra

Reem Acra

Reem Acra

RM

Roberto Cavalli

Stella McCartney

Valentino

Victoria Beckham

organizing
your wardrobe

adapting your space

Space seems to be a recurring issue in my line of work. No matter how large or how many cupboards somebody has, there never seems to be enough room. On quite a few occasions I have had to remind clients that I am the Practical Princess and not the fairy godmother, as it was physically impossible to fit all their clothes into the space available. I would love to have a magic wand, but unfortunately I don't! The only powers I might have are those obtained through experience and knowing how to maximize and use space to its best advantage.

Structurally, there will be elements in your wardrobe, cupboards or walk-in closet that you cannot move or alter. However, hanging rails can usually be repositioned and this will help you optimize your space and ensure that items have enough length to hang without getting crumpled.

Adjusting your hanging rails will give you a hanging length that suits your needs. Fitting two rails at different heights above one another in your wardrobe is another way to maximize your space. This is good for shorter items such as jackets, skirts and trousers and tops.

The pictures here and on the previous pages demonstrate how existing wardrobe space can easily be adapted. A shelf has been removed from this wardrobe and the hanging rail has been moved up to allow for an extra rail to be added below. This simple adjustment instantly doubles the wardrobe capacity and is ideal if you have lots of shorter items to hang. The beauty of this method is that it is not permanent, and if you wish to revert to the original configuration, the changes are easily reversible (don't chuck away the shelf).

If your cupboards are particularly wide or deep, double hanging rails one behind the other could be a consideration. However, you have to make sure that two hangers can sit side by side and fit comfortably in the wardrobe space so that your clothes will not be crushed.

Slanted wall hooks can be handy for hanging items in cupboards that are very shallow. Hidden dead space or small alcoves are also great places to fit these hooks if you have limited hanging space elsewhere.

Shelving is usually an inexpensive way of creating more space, and it is great for storing handbags, shoes, sweaters and so on. Extra shelves can often be added to existing wardrobes or cupboards, optimizing your storage space further.

If you don't have drawers inside your wardrobe, a free-standing drawer unit is a must. There are certain items that just have to live in a drawer, such as underwear, socks and sleepwear. And so many other items also benefit from being housed in a drawer, including T-shirts, clutch bags, gloves, belts, sunglasses… the list goes on and on.

WALK-IN WARDROBES

It is surprising how cheaply and easily one can make a walk-in closet out of a small spare room and easily be able to convert it back. By fixing rails onto the walls and/or using free-standing garment rails, a walk-in wardrobe-cum-dressing room will start to take shape. Extra storage such as shelving, trunks and chests of drawers can be added.

If you happen to be having built-in wardrobes fitted or making a permanent walk-in, here are a few tips to help you with your plan:

• Shelves should be movable. Make as many peg holes as possible, preferably every 10mm/½inch so that shelf heights can easily be adjusted. Make extra shelves, as you may need them.
• There are two ways to attach hanging rails: either beneath a shelf or directly to the sides of the wardrobe. It is essential that these are also adjustable.
• Measure the drop of your rehung clothes so that you know the width and height of hanging space you will need.
• Think about your drawer size and what you need to store in them. Drawers that are too deep can be counterproductive, because things can be lost and forgotten at the bottom.
• Think about the wardrobe doors. Sliding doors are space-saving, but they could stop you from viewing your clothes as a whole.

cleaning your space

When was the last time you took everything out of your wardrobe and gave it a really good clean? Go to your wardrobe, push your clothes to one side and run your finger along the hanging rail. It is more than likely that your fingertip will be covered in dust. Don't be horrified – you are not alone! I don't know why, but people rarely clean inside their wardrobes. We wouldn't eat off a dirty plate, so why would we hang clean clothes in a dusty wardrobe? You might not end up with food poisoning, but dust is made up partly from old skin cells – yuk!

When dust builds up it has a horrible stale smell and, before you know it, this will be impregnated into your clothes. Unfortunately, we get used to familiar smells around us and might not even notice this. I am not saying that your clothes smell, but it is worth keeping this in mind.

If there is a slight dusty smell, lemons cut in half, gently squeezed, covered with muslin and tied at the bottom will help to eradicate any unpleasant odours. The other trick is to use bowls of steaming water infused with an essence such as rose. Both of these solutions should be placed at the bottom of the wardrobe and changed when the water cools or the lemon becomes dry. Keep the wardrobe door closed and be careful that no item touches either of them.

I have used the boiling water tip for clothes that have been stored badly and had a particularly musty smell. I once made a mini-steam room in a small bathroom by filling the bath and sink with boiling water and essence to create a sauna-like effect. The clothes were hung on a hanging rail with spaces in between them and bowls of boiling water were placed beneath. The aroma from this was fantastic and the clothes smelt so much better.

A PROPER CLEAN

To clean your wardrobe properly, take everything out of your wardrobe and either dust it down with a dry cloth or use your vacuum cleaner to go over all the surfaces. Now go over everything with a damp cloth to remove all the dust and dirt. Once this has been done, use a cleaning product, preferably one that is lavender-based (make sure that it has no bleaching agent in it), to freshen up the wardrobe and leave a nice smell.

You must make sure that your wardrobe and rail is completely dry before you put your clothes back in, or staining could occur. It is also worth putting in a perfume bomb to keep the wardrobe fresh.

Drawers should be treated in the same way. Once they are spotless, line them with scented paper. Not only will this make drawers smell nice, but they will also be easier to clean next time around.

tools of the trade

HANGERS

Before you hang your clothes, consider for a moment what type of hanger you use. It is surprising how one can transform a wardrobe by simply hanging the clothes on matching hangers. When opening the wardrobe door, your eyes will no longer be focused on a sea of mismatched hangers all hanging at different levels. Your clothes will now seem to take on a new life and you will start to appreciate them again.

The type of hanger you choose is a lot more important than you may think. The biggest complaint is that most of the hangers listed below are responsible for the dreaded pointy shoulder.

WIRE

I call it the 'heroin' of hangers. This evil contraption may look harmless and your addiction to it may be because they don't take up much room and are free. Think again! Wire hangers easily become distorted, and clothes either hang on for dear life to the drooping shoulders or fall off completely. Another complaint is the coiled wire on the neck of the hanger, which can snag or tear delicate fabrics. Rust can also be an issue, and it is almost impossible to remove from clothes. The long-term damage to your clothes may be irreversible, and there is no rehab that can sort them out.

PADDED

For me, padded hangers are old-fashioned and have no place in a modern-day wardrobe. They also take up too much room, cutting hanging capacity by half. The fabric attracts dust and after time they split and become grubby.

WOODEN

Some wooden hangers are fabulous, but cheap ones often splinter, causing snags and pulls. Clothes also slip off easily if the hangers are highly varnished.

PLASTIC

Multicoloured plastic hangers can be offensive to the eye and look cheap, not doing justice to your lovely clothes. The shapes vary and can be too large or too small. They also snap easily and plastic splinters can occur.

The type of hanger you choose is a lot more important than you may think. The biggest complaint is that most of the hangers listed here are responsible for the dreaded pointy shoulder.

In the same way that your body fits your clothes, so should your hanger. My frustration at the lack of hangers to complement different garments led me to produce my own range. Key considerations for these products were:

- Movable shoulder span
- Non-slip
- Space-efficient and streamlined
- Contemporary
- Unisex
- Unobtrusive colour

I wanted my five-hanger family to sit at exactly the same height, so there would be no undulating effect.

SHIRT
This hanger is the most popular, used for shirts, tops, dresses, knitwear and, increasingly, jackets. This hanger can be gently moulded to the shape of your garment. It is great for knitwear, as it doesn't stretch it.

SUIT WITH BAR
Used for jackets and trouser suits. This hanger has contoured shoulders, so it can be used for most tailored clothing. The trousers should be hung over the bar with the waistband at the back of the jacket.

SUIT WITH CLIP
Designed for skirt suits and for dresses that need extra support, such as strapless or halter-necked evening dresses, for example. Long, heavy evening skirts can also be hung on these. For extra protection when hanging delicate fabrics, put a sheet of acid-free tissue paper under the pegs.

TROUSER
For trousers with a crease, line up the leg seams so that the trousers lay flat, then hang them with the seat pointing towards the open end of the hanger. For jeans and flat-fronted trousers or leggings, fold vertically in half with pockets on the outside (if they have them), with the gusset pointing towards the open end of the hanger. This will create a flat line, giving a uniform look.

SKIRT

Used for skirts and shorts. Before clipping the skirt onto the pegs, make sure any zips or buttons are done up, so that the garment lies flat when hung. These hangers are quite versatile and can also be used for hanging shawls, scarves and even boots. For extra protection when hanging delicate fabrics, put a sheet of acid-free tissue paper under the pegs.

HANGING RAIL

A hanging rail is not essential, but they are so, so useful. You can pick them up quite cheaply and the light, foldable type should be sufficient for your needs. A hanging rail will not only help when you start to reorganize your wardrobe, but it is also useful when you are packing to go away (see pages 122–125).

hanging your clothes by type and colour

To set about the task ahead, you will need to work from the list below. Your garments should already be in sections from when you tried on all your clothes. I now want you to start the process of rehanging and refolding everything in your beautifully clean wardrobe.

Remember that your space is an important criterion; sometimes we can't hang everything that we want to and it may be that, say, jeans will have to be folded, so I want you to start by hanging the non-foldable items. To make this easy for you, the garments to be hung are marked with an (h) on the list below. If you have a garment rail, it will help with the rehanging and colour-coordination process.

- Trousers (h)
- Skirts (h)
- Shirts and tops (h)
- Dresses (h)
- Suits (h)
- Coats (h)
- Jackets (h)
- Knitwear
- T-shirts and vests
- Loungewear

- Resort wear
- Outdoor and sportswear
- Jeans

Take each section, making sure that the appropriate hanger has been used as described on pages 50–55. To be honest, there is no right or wrong direction for your clothes to hang inside your wardrobe – it just comes down to personal preference – but you do need to ensure that all the garments face the same way. This will give your wardrobe a consistent flow.

One of the biggest no-nos is when the hanger hooks face towards you, as this will destroy the streamlined effect you are trying to create. It also takes longer to get your clothes out and you will often find yourself wrestling with the hanger and losing that calm feeling we are trying to achieve.

Now your clothes are hung and sectioned, I want you to colour coordinate them. You will not appreciate the difference this can make until you have seen the result. Put each section into colour groups and then grade them from the lightest to darkest. You will start to see a pattern emerge. There will be link pieces that will help you join the colours together – normally patterned or multicoloured pieces. Don't forget your blacks; textures or sleeve lengths will sit together in this group to give it its own order.

template folding

Whether your T-shirts, vests and sweaters sit on an open shelf or inside a drawer, template folding creates instant order, optimizes space and simply looks better.

You will first need to put your tops into sections – cardigans, V-necks, vests, T-shirts, long sleeves and so on. Once this is done, arrange the garments into colours, usually with the darkest at the bottom. You are ready to start folding.

Place your garment on a clean, flat surface with the front facing down. Now place the template in the centre with the base of the hole at the top of the

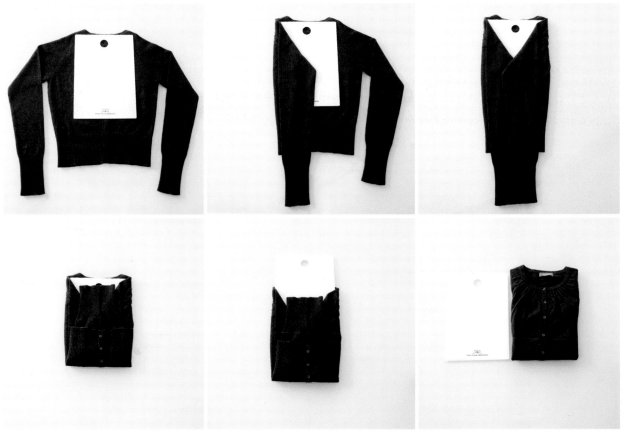

neckline. Fold in the left-hand side and then the right, making sure that any sleeves lie flat with the cuff pointing down to the bottom of the garment. Flip the bottom half up, and if any excess hangs over, fold it in. Gently pull the template out and turn your garment over. After repeating this process on all your garments, you will end up with an immaculate, equally sized pile.

lingerie

Lingerie drawers can be beautiful yet practical. You might think that this is taking organization a step too far, but when time is of the essence and your outfit depends on that nude strapless bra or that sexy lacy set you can't find, you may not think me so mad.

BRAS

Pop the bra cups together, pushing one into the other to create a dome, and then tuck the straps into the back of the cup. Make sure the cups are all facing the same way so that they nest neatly into one another. I prefer to keep bras in the dome shape, as it is more economical on space and great for keeping sets together. Pop the matching knickers behind the cup, then place the bras in straight lines, each one slightly overlapping the one behind, and arranging them by colour.

If you don't like the dome shape, lay your bra flat with the cups facing up and tuck all the straps behind. Any matching knickers can be put behind the cup. As with the domes, make sure you arrange the bras so that they are overlapping and by colour.

KNICKER FOLDING

There is nothing worse than a drawer full of knickers in a tangled mess. Drawer dividers are a great way to prevent this.

Place your knickers down with the bottom facing up, turn in the sides so that the gusset is pretty much even to the sides and then flip the knickers in half. They should now fit snugly into the drawer dividers or behind a matching bra. Alternatively, you can also lay them in the drawer and tier them in colours.

'MIRACLE' UNDERWEAR

'Miracle' underwear doesn't always do what it says on the packet. Bras without straps rarely have sufficient support; decorative nipple guards often highlight rather than hide and seams on control-top briefs, shorts and hosiery can often be unsightly. Be realistic about what you actually wear and edit anything that doesn't work. When you have your 'miracle' must-haves, place them all together so that they are easy to find.

NAUGHTY KNICKERS

If you want to conceal your naughty knickers, put them into satin bags – this will help hide them from any prying eyes and save your blushes! Don't, however, hide them too well in the depths of your wardrobe or drawers, or you might miss out on a moment of passion!

hosiery and socks

My mother is a champion sock folder – you may laugh, but it is true!
Socks were always folded in a flat, neat way. I have taken this
process and adopted it as my own. Here's how she folds them:

Place the two socks together, making sure that the heels are together, lay them flat and then fold in half. Take the cuff of one sock in your thumb and turn the remaining folds inside out. Your hand should still be inside the socks like a glove puppet. Hold the bottom and, using your other hand, straighten the fabric and flatten the inside folds; you should end up with a neat flat sock.

You can do the same with tights/pantyhose or longer socks. Carry out the same process, but with more folds. By doing this, your socks and tights will sit neatly in a drawer and also fit tidily into a drawer divider.

swimwear

Like knickers, swimwear tends to end up in a tangled mess, with bikini tops and bottoms getting separated from one another. To prevent this, the best way to keep them is in a bikini bag. Before Practical Princess manufactured its own bikini bags, we used ziplock sandwich bags to store swimwear. This is a great way to ensure that all swimwear sits together and the sets stay as a pair.

This system also makes packing for holidays or trips a lot easier. Bikini bags are handy to carry your damp or wet swimwear home from the beach or pool. Remember to take wet swimwear out afterwards though, because if it isn't washed and dried properly, the material could rot or perish.

shoes and boots

We all tend to have our favourite shoes and boots that we wear regularly; usually the same five or six pairs. It is likely that you don't even know how many pairs you own. Even if you are not the next Imelda Marcos, you probably have a lot more shoes than you think, including plenty of pairs that you rarely wear.

I definitely have my day-to-day favourites that I wear all the time, but I also have quite a few other shoes that only work with certain outfits. These rarely get an outing, but I need to keep them close to hand, as they are relevant to my wardrobe and it is important that I can find them quickly and easily.

I don't know how you store your shoes, but I have seen shoes and boots piled at the bottom of wardrobes, thrown under the bed, stacked in old shoe boxes and even scattered all over the house. At some point, most of us have been guilty of this behaviour. But if you keep your shoes like this, damage is certain to occur – anything from your shoes getting squashed and losing their shape to dust becoming ingrained in suede and satin fabrics, or stones and studs getting damaged or lost altogether.

I have learned so much about organizing, displaying and storing shoes by working for Tamara Mellon, the founder of Jimmy Choo. As you can imagine, her shoe and handbag collection is vast. Tamara has over 400 pairs of shoes in her current wardrobe with many more archived, and it is my job to make it easy for her to find any particular shoe.

To do this, I first organize them into style categories. These range from closed toe, peep toe, sandals, wedges, shoeboots, ankle boots, long boots and whatever other style is current. The styles are then colour coordinated and divided into material types – leather, skin, patent and so on. By doing this, any shoe style in a particular texture or colour is easy to find and the visual effect of all the shoes lined up on the shelves creates a boutique-like feel.

Very few people in the world have as many shoes as Tamara and Imelda. I use the same formula for all my clients, but I adapt my system according to what they have. As I do for Tamara, first separate your shoes into categories. Put all your flats together, arranging them in types, e.g. ballerinas, brogues, trainers, flip-flops and sandals. Do the same with your heels. I always keep all my flats on a two-tiered shoe rack at the bottom of my wardrobe for easy access, as I wear them daily.

All my other shoes are stored in Practical Princess shoe boxes with a photo-image on the front produced using our special software. The shoe boxes were specially designed with pull-out drawers because for years it had irritated me that stacked shoe boxes with a lid were impossible to access easily. I always seemed to want the shoes that were right in the middle or at the bottom of the pile of boxes. It was rare that I was able to retrieve them without the stack toppling over and the lids breaking. It would end with me having a temper tantrum and going out in trainers instead!

Shoe boxes are the best way to protect your shoes, especially ones you don't wear very much. I recommend that cardboard is used rather than plastic, so that the shoes can breathe. If you are going to store your shoes in boxes with photographs, then it is a good idea to stack them in categories and colours.

If you want to display your shoes on shelves or shoe racks, make sure that they are dusted regularly. As sad as I may sound, a feather duster does the job perfectly.

For your boots, plastic inserts will help ensure longevity, especially around the ankle. They also enable boots to stand up by themselves.

YSL

YSL

PRACTICAL PRINCESS

Alexander McQueen

PRACTICAL PRINCESS

Nicholas Kirkwood

PRACTICAL PRINCESS

Cleo B

PRACTICAL PRINCESS

Jimmy Choo

handbags

Like shoes, handbags can get a raw deal. They are often thrown into cupboards, stacked on top of each other or squashed so tightly that the original design takes on a new shape.

I often see handbags being kept in their dust bags, and although this will protect them, the chances of them being used are slim – as they say, 'out of sight is out of mind'.

I have coveted people's handbags and have seen how badly they have been treated. If only there was a 'handbag helpline' and some deserving owner could adopt them (ME!). If you don't want the bag police after you, here are a few tips.

If you visit any fashion website such as Net-a-Porter and look at the delicious handbags they sell, you will see that they have categorized them into a variety of different types: totes, shoulder bags, shoppers, clutches and so on. Different care is needed depending upon the type of bag.

TOTES AND SHOULDER BAGS
I quite often see totes with structured handles being distorted, as the shelves they are stored on are not deep enough. Make sure that the handles have room to stand – if space is limited, the bottom of your wardrobe could be the answer. Stuff the inside of the bag with old newspapers or tissue paper pushed into a plastic bag or dust cover. This will not only maintain the structure of the bag, but it also creates a ready-made removable bag shaper that you can use time and time again.

Most shoulder bags need a bag shaper, but there are a lot of bags around at the moment that are flat in shape. Everybody categorizes this shape differently, but for the sake of argument I will call it the 'shopper'. These don't

need to have any padding inside and should instead be laid flat or hung on a hook or handle, making a display feature.

CLUTCHES

Clutches come in all shapes and sizes, from the very large to the small and ornate. Shelves and drawers are the best place to store them. If possible, stand them up rather than laying them flat so that you will be able to see them more easily and damage is less likely to occur.

I quite often see handbags being kept in their dust bags, and although this will protect them, the chances of them being used are slim – as they say, 'out of sight is out of mind'.

Stuff the inside of the bag with old newspapers or tissue paper pushed into a plastic bag or dust cover. This padding will not only maintain the structure of the bag, but it also creates a ready-made removable bag shaper that you can use time and time again.

belts

Although I use quite a few different systems for storage, belts give me a headache because there are so many different shapes and sizes around.

You will be able to roll up or coil most of your belts. Keep the buckle on the outside and put an elastic band around the belt to prevent it from unravelling. Arrange your belts by type and colour. Drawers, boxes and trays are all good storage solutions.

Wide belts will vary because of their structure, and laying them flat is usually the best option.

Corset-style belts are structured and need to be stood upright. For a space-saving solution, put coiled belts inside.

Cummerbunds need to be gently folded. Don't use elastic bands to stop them unravelling; if need be, use ribbon.

Another way of storing belts is to hang them. Hooks and belt bars can make a great display feature and are easy to see at a glance. If your wardrobe is deep enough, you can always put these on the inside door of the cupboard, making sure that they will not catch on your clothes.

costume jewellery

I like to see chunky necklaces hung up, as I think they look gorgeous and it stops them from getting tangled, but this is not always practical. If you can, use the back of a door or a small section of wall. You will be able to fix hooks to hang and display your necklaces on. Double and triple hanging will save space and create an eclectic look.

If you don't want to hang your necklaces, an alternative method of storage is to place them in a drawer lined with a piece of suedette or velvet, which should be stuck down – double-sided tape will do the trick. This will stop the necklaces from slipping around and getting tangled up with other pieces.

Rings, earrings and brooches are best kept in jewellery boxes that are compartmentalized. My preference is Perspex trays that are subdivided and that can either be stacked on top of one another or placed inside drawers. Necklaces too can be kept in the same way, but be mindful of tangling. Bangles, bracelets and cuffs are easy to display on a kitchen roll/paper towel holder. Most good homeware stores sell them in a variety of styles.

hats

Hats seem to be the accessories that are often overlooked and forgotten about when organizing your wardrobe. It is worthwhile making them visible or accessible, as hats can totally transform a look rather than just collecting dust at the back of your wardrobe.

The good old-fashioned hat box is still a great way to store the traditional Ascot, wedding hat or fascinator. These are hats that we only take out occasionally, so it is best to keep them boxed. To help you identify them, stick a photograph or label on the box.

Everyday hats, such as a trilby or a flat shooting cap, can be stored on shelves, in drawers or hung from hooks. Baseball caps can be stacked, as can panamas, straws and trilbys. Hats, again, can make lovely visual displays.

scarves

There are so many different types of scarves. The majority can be folded and stacked on shelves or in drawers.

The ones that are usually problematic are the silky types. Some can simply be folded into a square – stack and stagger them so that you can see the different designs. Others, including the fine cashmere and cotton neck scarves that are popular at the moment, can be twisted and bunched to form a ball that can either be boxed or put away in a drawer.

the common clothes moth

Tineola bisselliella, otherwise known as the common clothes moth, is not your average sort of moth that is attracted to light; in fact, they hate it. These little devils are more likely to be found hiding in a dark corner of your wardrobe.

They are small and unobtrusive – only 6–8 mm/⅜ inch in length – with straw-coloured wings and no markings. In fact, they are rather elegant, like a champagne-coloured Concorde! The larvae are creamy white with a brown head and can be up to 10mm/½ inch long. The adult moths don't feed on fabrics, but the female moth lays eggs that hatch out larvae that will feed on your clothes, leaving a tracery of irregular holes. The clothes moth can hide under floorboards, carpets, upholstered furniture, air ducts and antique furniture, and even in felt in pianos.

I've had moths, and if you've had them too, boy do I sympathize! I was verging on an epidemic and am still not quite sure how I got them, but I figure it was through purchasing vintage clothes. If only I had kept them sealed in a bag or taken them straight to the dry-cleaners, I might have saved myself a lot of time and money. I tried all the tips and tricks available, but nothing seemed to work. In desperation, feeling defeated by these evil invaders, I turned to a pest control company to save my sanity and my clothes.

Before they would come to fumigate, I had to dry-clean and launder all the clothes in the house, including sheets, towels, bedding and cuddly toys. You name it, I cleaned it! The whole house was filled with plastic bin liners and boxes, as everything had to be sealed after being washed and dried to prevent further infestation. I actually gave up on what I looked like because it was virtually impossible to get dressed.

After the house was sprayed – which included curtains, carpets and sofas – and I was given the go-ahead to put everything back, I cleaned the house like a woman obsessed. Although financially broke from my huge dry-cleaning and

pest-control bill, and exhausted from all the cleaning, washing and ironing, there was a deep sense of satisfaction. I had killed those darn moths, and the house had never been so shiny!

Even though I hope that this never happens to you, I have learned valuable first-hand experience from this drama and it has helped me at work. It has enabled me to tackle moth problems practically and also to understand the emotional impact it has on my clients when these pests attack.

PREVENTION

It is difficult to keep moths at bay, but there are ways of combating them:

• Vintage and second-hand clothing must be cleaned before bringing it home.
• The same goes for second-hand or antique furniture and rugs or carpets.
• Regularly vacuum and clean under beds, skirting boards and furniture.

- Change your vacuum bag often, as this is a breeding ground.
- Clean out the inside of your closet/drawers/cupboards with a bleach-free detergent on a monthly basis (lavender-based products are good).
- Don't put away dirty or soiled clothes. The moths prefer dirty fabric and are particularly attracted to clothing that contains human sweat or other liquids.
- Check and shake garments periodically (lint rollers can help).
- Mothballs are the old-fashioned way of keeping clothes free from moths. However, they are toxic, smell horrid and are unsafe around young children and pets.
- Cedar balls can be effective for the smaller moth larvae, but are not effective for the larger larvae and don't have as much effect as people think.
- Use moth-prevention sachets (including lavender-based products – there are many eco-friendly products on the market).

HOW TO GET RID OF MOTHS
- Dry-cleaning
- Washing clothes in water above the temperature of 50°C/120°F. (I cannot guarantee it, but I have hand-washed things at much lower temperatures and found that this has done the trick.)
- Freezing. This can be used for garments such as cashmere or delicate fabrics that cannot be washed in hot water. Just put the item in a plastic bag and pop it into the freezer for a day.
- Hang items out in bright sunlight. (This might be better for a rug or blankets. I have only used this as a precaution and in conjunction with a lint roller.)
- If you have a really bad infestation, call in the professionals. All companies have different methods of how to combat moth infestation, but most of them use powerful insecticides to kill off the moths.

identifying the gaps

By now, your clothes should be hung in sections and colour coordinated, and as a result, your wardrobe or space will have a very different feel and look. The process that you have just carried out is not just about making your wardrobe look ordered and beautiful, but preparing you for the next stage. By looking at what is left in your wardrobe and cupboards, you should easily be able to identify any patterns such as repeat buys.

When I am working with a client, this is the best time to compile a practical and realistic shopping list. Whether the client is shopping alone or with me, the list will help prevent any impulse buying and constrain magpie behaviour.

When putting your shopping list together, it is essential to keep your wardrobe

assessment in mind and to remember what your goal is. By looking back through your wardrobe, you should be able to identify the gaps.
Do you need any of the following?

BASICS
The cement of your wardrobe: vests, T-shirts, leggings, cardigans and so on, in generic colours (these need to be updated regularly.)

FOUNDATION PIECES
These are the hard-working building blocks of your wardrobe that need to integrate and complement one another in colour. Foundation pieces should include skirts, trousers, jeans, jackets, coats and dresses.

FASHION UPDATE
This could be anything from an accessory to the latest trend in jeans. These items help us to keep our look fresh each season.

LOUNGEWEAR
These are clothes that are comfortable and easy to wear, and that you still look good in, whether you are at home or in the park.

RESORT WEAR
From swimwear to cover-ups, beach hats and sun dresses.

LINGERIE
Strapless bras and seam-free knickers in nude, blacks and whites. The other stuff is up to you!

SHOES AND BAGS
A quick way to update your wardrobe. Make sure that they work for your everyday life. Don't go for the small clutch bag or the pole-dancing shoes that you can't walk in until you have the essentials in place.

ACCESSORIES
A good way to update your wardrobe is with belts, jewellery and scarves, making your look more current.

EVENT WEAR
Something suitable for a wedding, a christening, a day at the races, a glam party, a prize-giving ceremony or even the Oscars to pick up your award!

LINK PIECE
You love it… but you can't wear it because you don't have the right things to go with it.

By identifying what is missing and keeping in mind your lifestyle needs, you should be able to compile a shopping list quite easily. Before you get carried away, you must start with the boring essentials – your basics. No fun, I know – after all, who wants to spend their hard-earned cash on a plain white vest or a black cardigan? It kinda kills that buzz when you get home and empty your bags and there is nothing exciting to show anyone. But, as boring as they may seem, these are the items that are going to tie your everyday look together. Missing or tired pieces from your basic collection can weaken an outfit or sometimes prevent it from working at all.

Foundation pieces are every bit as important as the basics. They are the hard-working building blocks that help to create your style. Essential to your wardrobe, they will be the foundation of your look. They may have a fashion

element, but tend to sit on the classical side. These are pieces that we can wear to death without the risk of being a one-outfit wonder. This is because they can both be worn together and mixed and matched with the rest of your wardrobe.

Each of us will require different foundation pieces to suit our needs. For me and my lifestyle, my foundation pieces will include good jeans that I can wear to work, a couple of tailored and leather jackets, a pencil skirt and a few transitional dresses that will take me from day to night. These items will allow me to dress with ease for my day-to-day life.

Once you have got the staples listed, you can start to add your own touches. These are items that have a personal appeal or fit your own particular style. By adding shoes, bags and accessories or anything else from the list provided, you should have the basis of a well-balanced shopping list.

going shopping

The moral of this story is that you will be more successful when you go out shopping if you look good and feel confident.

looking good and feeling confident

Without wanting to sound like the headmistress of an old-fashioned finishing school, there are some rules that you should stick to when it comes to going shopping. From my own experience, I know that if I look and feel good, I am more successful when I shop. It may not seem important to look your best when you go shopping, but I have witnessed clients having a meltdown when they don't feel confident.

Let me give you an example. I was shopping with a lady for spring/summer wear. Bear in mind that this was mid-February in the UK, right at the beginning of the shopping season.

Like most, after a long winter with covered legs, hers were not looking their best. This made her reluctant to try on dresses and skirts. When she finally did try on a skirt, she sheepishly came out of the changing room. To my horror, she was still wearing her American Tan knee-highs. Not a good look! Luckily, when I pulled up my trousers to expose my pasty pins, she could see the funny side!

The moral of this story is that you will be more successful when you go out shopping if you look good and feel confident. This also applies when it comes to online shopping and trying on goods at home. As obvious as these points may seem, here is a little checklist:
• Wax, shave or depilate your legs and, if you're buying swimwear, do your bikini line.
• If you like yourself with a golden glow, put on a little fake tan.
• If you usually wear make-up, put some on.
• Remember, your hair is your biggest accessory – make it look fabulous.
• Wear good underwear – not your frou-frou lacy stuff, as this will show through clothes, but seamless nude knickers and a strapless T-shirt bra.
• Wear sensible clothes and shoes that are easy to get on and off.
• Wear layers because shops can vary in temperature. There is nothing worse than being too hot or too cold, as it will affect your concentration.

what to take with you

Looking good is not the only key to successful shopping. You will need to take some things with you. I don't want you to be weighed down with bags before you start, but a few things are necessary.

I am not going to ask you to take a pair of high heels with you, as some shops will provide them for you try to on with clothes, or if they don't, you can improvise and stand on your tiptoes.

What I do want you to take are any items that need things to go with them. Trying to remember colours, textures and shapes is impossible, and even with the best eye in the world, the brain can play tricks on you.

Make sure that you remember to take your written shopping list with you. It is all too easy to forget things that you need to buy. Keep your budget in mind, and leave your emergency credit card at home!

where to go

Where you live and what your budget is will determine where you shop. Your shopping list will also influence where you go.

Shops on high streets, designer avenues, malls and department stores always sit in a cluster. With everything in close proximity and a choice to suit all budgets, this is a great place to start. This is usually the best place to find basics and foundation pieces, so try to do this first rather than leaving them until the end of the day. I cannot emphasize the importance of these pieces enough! Not only will your wardrobe not work without them, but they will

come in useful throughout the day when trying on new pieces. If you blow your budget before you buy these essentials, you will regret it!

Designer jeans brands have exploded onto the market as they have become a must in most women's wardrobes. It is acceptable today even for boardroom executives to wear a pair of jeans with a tailored jacket. Specialist jeans shops have started to pop up everywhere. My personal favourite is Donna Ida in London. Thanks to her large selection of all the latest jeans and encyclopedic knowledge of denim, I rarely need to go elsewhere.

There are other places such as independent boutiques, one-off designer stores and markets where you can pick up unique pieces to personalize your look. Vintage fashion is a great way to get an original look. This trend is so popular and there are many shops around. Some people really suit this style and are good at spotting gems. If this is not your forte, be careful – just because it is vintage doesn't make it cool. You may end up looking like you have raided your childhood dressing-up box!

Designer resale shops are not only there to get rid of unwanted things. They can also be a fab place to pick up a designer bargain. Most shops will only take barely worn or unworn pieces, so you are sure to get a nearly new item at a fraction of the price.

Designer outlets have become more and more prominent in the last decade. From outlet malls to discount retailers such as TK Maxx, reasonably priced fashion is accessible to all. Most of these stores are situated on the outskirts of towns and are not always that easy to get to. If you can't get to one, go online and have a look at theoutnet.com or eBay's fashion outlet. There is a flipside to this sort of shopping – just because something is a bargain doesn't mean that you have to buy it. Do you really need it? Is it on your list?

Sales seem to start earlier and earlier these days. This makes shopping difficult, as it is almost as if we have to buy a season ahead, picking up summer dresses in February and winter coats in August. Unfortunately, unless you shop at the beginning of the season, you might discover that your size is sold out, and find yourself scrabbling through rails of reduced-price clothes and coming out empty-handed. There are of course huge positives to the sales. As they start mid-season nowadays, you are often able to pick up the latest trends and enjoy them immediately at a knock-down price.

If you are at all uncertain about your purchase, it is crucial that you check the refund policies. These vary so much, with some stores not giving refunds at all and only offering a credit note. Markets, vintage stores and second-hand designer shops might not even offer that. You will need your receipt if you want to return an item. A good tip is to keep your receipts in your wallet, not in the shopping bag, to reduce the chance of losing them.

inside the store

This can be really daunting for some people. Clients have explained that when they shop alone everything turns into a blur. The clothes become a mass of colour and items all blend into one. I understand that feeling and have experienced this sensation myself in large stores.

The best way to combat this feeling is to break the space down and pick a small section to start with. Methodically work your way around the shop floor, ensuring that you look at everything in turn, and this will prevent a frenzied supermarket sweep approach.

Most shops are divided into sections and these will be split into fashion stories, designers or garment types. Using the sections as a guide will help to keep you focused and then you won't feel so overwhelmed.

HANGER APPEAL

As you work your way through these little sections, your eye will be drawn to deliberately positioned temptations, quite often on a mannequin. These are meant to lure you in, just as if you were a child in a sweet shop.

Some of these pieces will definitely be worth trying on, but don't overlook the less obvious pieces. Sometimes these items may have little or no hanger appeal, but they will come to life when you try them on and will become the foundation pieces of your wardrobe.

Clothes that are folded will look the same. Take the time to explore these items, as they will inevitably vary in shape and style and you don't want to miss a hidden gem.

the dreaded changing room

Most changing rooms have a policy of six items or fewer and it can be aggravating if you have more than this number of items to try on. The best way to work round this is to logically sort your choices – for example, keep all dresses and jumpsuits together, as they do not require a separate. This will also allow you to compare similar styles so that you find the strongest piece. If you have chosen lots of tops, make sure that you have trousers or a skirt to try them on with.

As you eliminate items, you will be able to bring new pieces into the changing room. Make sure that the attendant knows what you still have to try on, as I have experienced untried items being put back prematurely.

Some attendants are there to give you advice and help you with your decisions. I don't want to give them a bad name, but they can sometimes flatter you into buying something that's not quite right, especially when their commission is on the line.

TRYING ON

Bad lighting, mirrors coming at you in every direction and you have just noticed a new piece of cellulite or flab you didn't realize you had – I am sure we can all identify with this scenario. Braving a shop changing room can be a challenging experience, but rest assured that all women feel the same, no matter how comfortable they are with their body.

I don't want to lecture you on body shapes and sizes, and what will suit you best. There are enough books and magazine articles out there doing this, and I am still not convinced that by following every rule you will get the best results.

One of the things that I have observed from being in changing rooms with my clients is that they tend to stand far too close to the mirror, studying the parts of their body they hate. Ask yourself this question: when you look at someone, do you look at them as a whole or do you zoom in on one particular part? I look at a person as a whole and that is what you need to do too.

When I am shopping with my clients, I am there to be objective, ensuring that the fit and proportions are correct, and that the piece in question is flattering. As I am not in the changing room with you, here's what to do.

Stand way back from the mirror (a couple of metres/five or six feet, if possible), even if this means coming out of the changing room and finding another mirror. Although you may not be comfortable doing this, you have more chance of seeing yourself as others do. It will give you a general overview to see whether the style does suit and flatter.

CONSIDERATIONS
• Are you standing properly? Shoulders back, tummy in, long neck and head high?
• Think about the whole outfit. If you don't have the right shoes, visualize heels by standing on your tiptoes.
• Remember to take off socks or tights/pantyhose if they are not part of the outfit, otherwise it will kill the look.
• Try to be objective and not negative. Do your proportions look reasonably balanced? Or is this outfit/garment cutting your shape up?
• Am I wearing the outfit or is the outfit wearing me? Sometimes less is more.

Having this distance will enable you to see whether the dreaded body part really is that prominent. This can help you change how you perceive yourself.

You do now need to walk closer to the mirror again, but don't stand too close – about a metre/two to three feet away. This is to check the details – to see whether your lines are smooth, and that nothing is pulling or gaping. Sometimes 'miracle' underwear (including bras) can help, so don't forget to wear them or take them with you. Risking it and leaving it to your imagination usually ends in disappointment and a return visit to the shops.

your style

Have you ever wondered how your look or style has been shaped? Our look is not only influenced by fashion magazines, celebrity icons, music and art, but often – without us even knowing it – by our friends and peers too.

Unconsciously, most of us wear a uniform, but not the type we wore at school where everybody looked identical. If you look around the streets, you will notice that groups tend to model themselves on one another. This happens across the board, from teenage girls and boys to pensioners. Of course, some people are completely unique and individual, and stand out from the crowd.

If you want to evolve your look and keep it fresh, here's how to do it:
• When looking through magazines, be realistic – are you looking at the model or the clothes? Place your thumb over the model's face and see if you still like the outfit.
• Strip your look back, playing around with accessories – this is the quickest way to update and change your look.
• Think about your hair – you wear it everyday and it can dramatically change your image.
• Don't be scared to try things on – you might be surprised at what actually suits you.
• Adapt a trend so that you feel comfortable in it – you don't have to go the whole hog and looks can be mixed.
• If the key colours of the season don't suit you, you can always wear them away from your face or as an accessory.
• Don't overlook make-up, because this can really change a look, as can eyebrows and skin tone.
• Less is more. If in doubt, keep it simple – minimalism is always a success.
• You don't have to stick to one look. Have fun with clothes – fashion changes and so can you!
• Project your personality through your style.

shopping for special occasions

This can be one of the most stressful types of shopping. No matter how long we have to prepare, we often end up leaving it to the very last minute.

Special occasion outfits are usually a one-hit wonder. The formality or the dress code limits what we can wear, and we want to look our best. Whether it's for a christening, a wedding, the races or the party of the year, special occasions are when we often become impulsive and lose our senses. Try not to do this, as the item you buy will inevitably end up not being worn again. Instead, aim to be more timeless in your choices: block colours and simple clean lines tend not to date and are more versatile. Build a look with accessories: hats, gloves, jewellery, shoes and handbags.

Going to the hairdressers for these events can make you feel a million dollars. Hairpieces can really add drama and glamour as well, but make sure that the person who is doing your hair is experienced. A spray tan and professional make-up will also help create that wow factor. When I need extra assistance for special events, I use a London-based company called InParlour, as they come to my home and save me valuable time. I have also used the in-store make-up services at MAC and various other cosmetic companies in the past.

My top tip for having professional make-up applied is to always start with a more natural look. The worst thing is staring at yourself in the mirror and not recognizing your own reflection. It is important to feel comfortable and confident. Remember, it is easier to build a look up than to try and tone it down.

packing

We all have different packing habits. Some of us will pack a week or two in advance, while others will still be packing when they should be on their way to the airport. Both of these approaches have their downfalls. If you pack your bag too early, you may find that you forget what you have put in and throw in unnecessary extras. Favourite items that you have packed but then want to wear leading up to your holiday will be pulled out of your case. But chucking everything in a case at the last minute means you will almost certainly pack too much or too little. Nothing will go together, and the creased and mismatched items will give you a unique holiday look!

BE PREPARED

The destination and length of your trip will determine what you need to pack. Lay out in advance what you think you will require and what you would like to take. Think about how many outfits you will realistically need and make sure that each outfit can be completed by mixing and matching. Don't forget to lay out lingerie, sleepwear, sportswear and so on – you would be surprised how easy it is to forget these items. You may find that you have put out far too much. We all do it. Be realistic and go back over your choices to decide what you actually need. A garment rail can be very useful during the process: you will be able to assess how well your holiday wardrobe works together.

If you need to cut back on accessories, metallic shoes, handbags and belts are a great way to lighten the load, as they tend to go with most colours.

Think about the time of day you will arrive and what you will be doing when you get there. Set aside what you will first need to wear – a bikini for the beach, for example, a ski suit for the slopes or pyjamas for bed. These should be packed at the top of your case for easy access when you arrive. This will stop you rummaging through your perfectly packed case and creasing all your clothes.

HOW TO PACK

Make sure that everything is clean and pressed before you start. A square wheelie case is preferable because the rigid sides reduce the chance of creasing. Lay the more structured clothes flat at the bottom – the fewer folds, the better. Use tissue paper to separate and protect your clothes from other items that can scratch or damage them. Once these are all in, you can pack your next layer. This will be the foldable items like T-shirts, jeans, shorts and so on. Fill any spaces with small items such as socks and underwear to create a solid base for your next layer. Shoes should be bagged and placed around the edges of the case, and bulky items such as handbags, toiletries, leather jackets and waterproofs can then be placed in the middle.

I like to take the majority of my toiletries and cosmetics in my hand luggage, but many airlines impose security regulations when it comes to carrying liquids onto the plane. If in doubt, check with your airline, as it is infuriating having your favourite perfume confiscated when going through security. When it

comes to toiletries, do try not to buy up the chemist shop/drugstore before you leave. You can always stock up at the airport or when you arrive.

UNPACKING

The last thing most of us want to do when arriving at our destination is unpack our suitcase. Here's where that little bit of preparation really comes into its own. You are ready to go and can grab whatever you need from the top of your case, leaving the unpacking until later.

This does not mean that you can leave it until mid-holiday. It is important to unpack as early as you can so that any creases can drop out. If you find that certain items look like a well-weathered face, hang them in the bathroom so creases can drop out in the steam.

index

credits

The author and publisher would like to thank the following designers, boutiques and businesses for their help with photography for this book:

Lucy in Disguise
10–13 King Street
London WC2E 8HN
020 7240 6590
www.lucyindisguiselondon.com
Pages 2, 85 right, 96 above left, 105, 107, 112, 113, 114, 117

Donna Ida
106 Draycott Avenue
London SW3 3AE
020 7225 3816
chelsea@donnaida.com
www.donnaida.com
Pages 106, 109, 111

9 London
www.9london.co.uk
Dress from 9 London on page 16 above left

Philip Treacy London
69 Elizabeth Street
London SW1W 9PJ
+44 (0) 207 730 3992
studio@philiptreacy.co.uk
www.philiptreacy.co.uk
Hat by Philip Treacy on page 86

Agent Provocateur
www.agentprovocateur.com

La Senza Lingerie
www..lasenza.co.uk

Jimmy Choo
www.jimmychoo.com

Net-a-Porter
www.net-a-porter.com

Topshop
www.topshop.com

Anthology Boutique
511 Old York Road
London SW18 1TF
07947 467385
anthology@live.co.uk

Make-up by **Amanda Harrington @ InParlour**
www.inparlour.co.uk
020 7736 7713
info@inparlour.co.uk

Hair by **Darren Hau**
07979 081522
darrenhau@hotmail.com
Celebrity, session, catwalk, photographic, TV

Kynance Dry Cleaning & Laundry
2–3 Kynance Place
London SW7 4QS
020 7584 7846

Portrait on page 12 by David Daughton

The publisher would like to thank those who kindly allowed us to photograph their wonderful homes and wardrobes, including Emily Evans and Grainne Stevenson. We also wish to thank our models, Alex, Anna, Clare, Darren, Emily, Karim and Maddie.

acknowledgments

There are so many people I need to thank for their help and assistance in getting this book to print, but Maisie, my beloved daughter, has to come top of the tree. Seeing the way she has fought her own battles since a baby and the achievements she has made has given me the strength to fight on when I felt that things were not going to plan. I am so proud of her – thank you, Angel.

I must then thank my mum, who has been the biggest role model in my life. Her hard work, love and determination have inspired me. She is the 'Practical Queen'. I must also thank her for the hard work she put in on the book. My dad, Poppie, must also be thanked, for always believing in me and instilling in me the belief that there is nothing I cannot do.

What would I have done with out the help of my assistant, Anna Hitchins – a truly talented young lady. She has worked tirelessly beside me, though tears and laughter, compiling this book. Thank you Anna – you are a star!

I would also like to thank my cousin Debbie and my wonderful friends, especially Hannah Coleman, Gilly Smith, Emily Evans, Maddie Farley, Waggi and Simon, who have had to listen to numerous readings and have helped me in so many ways. The list goes on, but I must not forget Grainne Stevenson, Claire Arden, Angie Robinson, Olivia White and Victoria Stephenson.

I would also like to thank Tamara Mellon, because of her faith in me and for all her help with Practical Princess.

To all at RPS a big thank you, especially Alison Starling for approaching me and giving me the opportunity to write the book, Annabel Morgan for being kind about my writing ability, Leslie Harrington for allowing me to use my own creative visualization and Polly Wreford and her assistant Sarah for such beautiful photography and interpreting my vision.